# CLASSICAL

## SOUNDS OF MUSIC

David and Patricia Armentrout

The Rourke Corporation, Inc.
Vero Beach, Florida 32964

PHOTO CREDITS:
© Armentrout: cover, pages 7, 10, 12; © Hal Kern/Intl. Stock: title page; © Oscar C. Williams: page 4; © Hirz/Archive Photos: page 8; © Sue Anderson: page 13; © Kay L. Hendrich: page 15; © Hackett/Archive Photos: page 17; © Archive Photos: page 18; © Peter Tenzer Studio, Inc./Intl. Stock: page 21


PRODUCED BY:
East Coast Studios, Merritt Island, Florida


EDITORIAL SERVICES:
Susan Albury

**Library of Congress Cataloging-in-Publication Data**

Armentrout, David. 1962-
     Classical / by David and Patricia Armentrout.
        p.  cm. — (Sounds of music)
     Includes bibliographical references (p. 24) and index.
     Summary: Brief text explores how music evolved from the baroque to the classical style, discussing instruments, famous composers, and the orchestra.
     ISBN 0-86593-534-3
     1. Music—History and criticism Juvenile literature.  [1. Music—History and criticism.]  I. Armentrout, Patricia, 1960-  II. Title.  III. Series
ML3928.A75  1999
781.6'8—dc21                                        99-14249
                                                                      CIP

# TABLE OF CONTENTS

## WHAT IS MUSIC?

Music is many things. A bird chirping is music. A poem sung to a **tune** (TOON), as in a nursery rhyme, is music. Piano playing is music. Music is also the sound of many instruments played at the same time.

Music comes in many styles. Some music is loud and bold; some music is soft and pleasing. Some music can make you feel sad, and some can lift your spirits high!

What is music to your ears?

*A flutist and violinist make beautiful music together.*

## CLASSICAL MUSIC

Do you know what classical music is? Maybe you have heard the term, but never really knew what it meant.

Classical music is a style of music. It was written, or **composed** (kum POZD), in a time in history called the classical period. The classical period was roughly between the years 1750 and 1825. If composers today create music in the same style, it is also called classical.

Music changes with time. Music writers, called composers, often study and learn from earlier writers. Classical composers made many changes to earlier music.

*Take time to enjoy the sounds of classical music.*

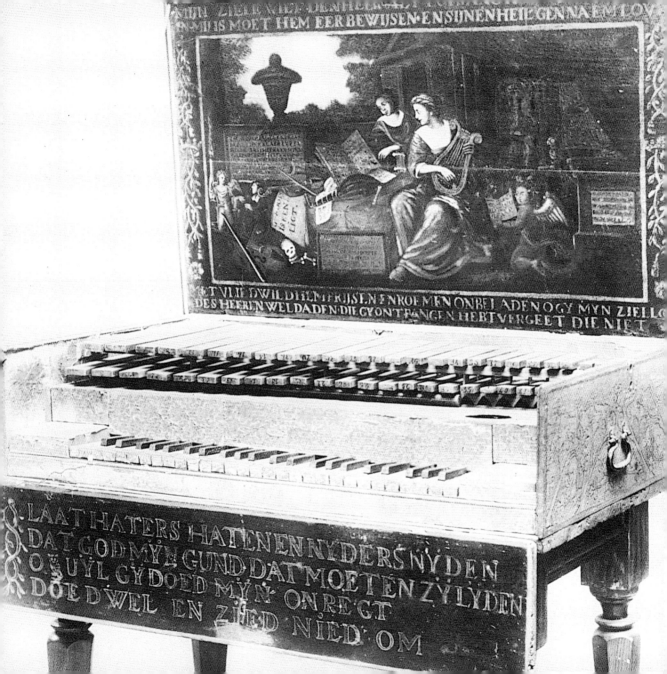

# BAROQUE PERIOD

The **baroque** (buh ROKE) period (1600-1750) in music was before the classical period. Baroque music is very fancy. Most baroque period music was written for the church or for the very rich and noble.

The **clavichord** (KLAV uh kord) and the **harpsichord** (HARP seh kord) are two early keyboard instruments. They were played during the baroque period.

Much of the baroque music included singing. It was heard in church and opera. An opera is a play that is sung.

*This eighteenth-century piano had steel plates instead of strings.*

# MUSIC CHANGES

In the mid 1700s music changed. The classical period in music began. Classical music is less fancy than baroque music. Classical sounds are more simple and clear.

Instruments became more important than song during the classical years. The piano took the place of older keyboards.

Composers gave private music lessons during the classical period. Many performed in public concerts, too. Music was no longer just for the church or for the rich and the noble.

*A student practices for a holiday program.*

a *flute are opened and closed to produce different tones.*

*A modern harp has 46 strings.*

## MUSIC CLASS

Some school children attend music class as early as kindergarten. A first music class can include singing songs and making simple instruments.

What do you learn in music class? Elementary children can learn to read music and play instruments. Often a class will perform in musical programs at school.

Older students are taught music history. Some lessons include interesting facts about classical composers.

*This music class prepares for a school performance.*

# MOZART

Imagine playing keyboards at 3, violin at 6, and conducting your own music by age 7. Wolfgang Amadeus Mozart did just that!

As a child, Mozart traveled to big European cities and performed concerts with his sister. As a teenager, Mozart composed operas and complex music pieces called **symphonies** (SIMP fuh neez).

Mozart wrote 18 operas and 40 symphonies during his life, and died when he was only 35. He was a musical genius. Mozart is considered one of the world's most gifted composers.

*Wolfgang Amadeus Mozart*
*at age six.*

# BEETHOVEN

Ludwig van Beethoven's life story is very interesting. Although he suffered many hardships, Beethoven continued to write music.

Beethoven's mother and sister died when he was a boy. Beethoven's father, who treated him poorly, was left to raise him.

Beethoven also suffered from a hearing loss caused by a childhood illness. Beethoven eventually went deaf. Yet Beethoven composed and played some of his best music without hearing a single note!

*A portrait of the great German composer Ludwig van Beethoven.*

# ORCHESTRA

An **orchestra** (OR kuh stra) is a group of instruments that are played together. Orchestras often play music written by the great classical composers.

An orchestra has four basic sections. The string section includes violins, violas, cellos, and double **basses** (BAY sis). The woodwind section includes instruments such as flutes and clarinets. Trumpets, trombones, and tubas are part of the brass section. Drums, cymbals, and piano are in the percussion group. Many orchestras also have a harp.

*Each section of the orchestra sits together when they play.*

# MUSIC AROUND US

Have you heard a live performance of classical music? Many big cities have orchestras or symphonies. Maybe you have gone to a musical concert at school.

You don't need to go far to hear music. Music is all around us. Music is on the radio and television. You can buy all kinds of music from a music store.

Your local library has music, too. Not only do libraries offer books about music, they also allow you to explore the sounds of music with tapes and CDs.

# GLOSSARY

**baroque** (buh ROKE) — a style of art and music popular between 1600 and 1750 AD

**bass** (BASE) — the largest instrument in the string section

**clavichord** (KLAV uh kord) — a stringed keyboard instrument popular in the baroque era

**composed** (kum POZD) — written or arranged in an organized musical form

**harpsichord** (HARP seh kord) — an early keyboard instrument that produces sound by plucking its strings

**orchestra** (OR kuh stra) — a group of instruments organized to play music

**symphony** (SIMP fuh nee) — complex written music that is meant to be played by a full orchestra

**tune** (TOON) — a series of pleasing musical tones

# INDEX

# FURTHER READING

Find out more about music with these helpful books:

• Ardley, Neil. *Eyewitness Books: Music.* Knopf, 1989
• McLin, Lena. *Pulse: A History of Music.* Kjos West, 1977
• Montgomery, June, and Maurice Hinson. *Meet the Great Composers.* Alfred Publishing, 1995
• Spence, Keith. *The Young People's Book of Music.* Millbrook Press, 1995
• Ulrich, Homer. *"Classical Period in Music."* Grolier Multimedia Encyclopedia, 1998